Make Money at Craft Shows

A Guide for Crafters

Russ & Shirley Searle

Order this book online at www.trafford.com/08-0548
or email orders@trafford.com

Most Trafford titles are also available at major online book retailers.

© Copyright 2009 Russ and Shirley Searle.

All rights reserved. No part of this publication may be reproduced, stored in a retrieval system, or transmitted, in any form or by any means, electronic, mechanical, photocopying, recording, or otherwise, without the written prior permission of the author.

Cartoons by Nick Watkins

Note for Librarians: A cataloguing record for this book is available from Library and Archives Canada at www.collectionscanada.ca/amicus/index-e.html

Printed in Victoria, BC, Canada.

ISBN: 978-1-4251-7716-4

We at Trafford believe that it is the responsibility of us all, as both individuals and corporations, to make choices that are environmentally and socially sound. You, in turn, are supporting this responsible conduct each time you purchase a Trafford book, or make use of our publishing services. To find out how you are helping, please visit www.trafford.com/responsiblepublishing.html

Our mission is to efficiently provide the world's finest, most comprehensive book publishing service, enabling every author to experience success. To find out how to publish your book, your way, and have it available worldwide, visit us online at www.trafford.com/10510

Trafford
PUBLISHING

www.trafford.com

North America & international
toll-free: 1 888 232 4444 (USA & Canada)
phone: 250 383 6864 ♦ fax: 250 383 6804
email: info@trafford.com

The United Kingdom & Europe
phone: +44 (0)1865 487 395 ♦ local rate: 0845 230 9601
facsimile: +44 (0)1865 481 507 ♦ email: info.uk@trafford.com

10 9 8 7 6 5 4 3 2

Foreword

Craft shows are popular in North America because they harken back to the days when everything was made locally. Businesses strove for excellence in workmanship because satisfied and loyal customers paid their wages. Today the majority of clothing, jewellery, and all manner of handcrafted and food items are imported. Too many businesses are only interested in the bottom line. Product quality is a secondary consideration. Go into any mall or department store, and the variety and quality of goods offered have a sameness that can't be disguised by different brand names. They lack originality and variety. Customer service, once the cornerstone of retail businesses, is only paid lip service.

That's why craft fairs are more popular than ever. Customers know they will find a variety of well-made gifts, toys, foods, and art at these shows. They know they are buying directly from the handcrafter, and that this person is very interested in serving them. This makes the customer feel important.

Craft shows provide an opportunity for crafters and artists to showcase their skills and products. However, this doesn't mean a crafter can just show up and that customers will buy everything she puts on her table. The crafter has to know how to attract and serve customers.

The goods in traditional businesses may lack the variety and quality of the past, but retail advertising budgets have continued to grow, and merchants have always understood how to merchandise. To put this another way, there is a lot of competition for the retail dollar, and there are tips and tricks to attracting customers. Fortunately they're easy to learn.

Merchandising, selling and advertising are poorly understood by too many crafters, and this book is designed to help them compete in today's marketplace by enhancing their skills in these areas. Finally, we have included a small section on record keeping and accounting. This section won't show you how to set up your books—you'll need an accountant or bookkeeper for that—but it will clearly describe the difference between gross profit and net profit, and will give you some tips on setting a price for your crafts.

For many of us, achieving excellence in our creative endeavours provides a sense of fulfillment. Being rewarded by successfully selling these products of our own talent is the icing on the cake. This book is all about the icing.

Acknowledgments

If we tried to list all of our fellow crafters who assisted us with their tips, tricks, and comments, we would undoubtedly leave someone out. And that would be a shame since their help was invaluable. It would be like trying to thank everyone in our family for their help since many crafters have become our extended family. We see each other at the same shows, we endure the same privations and shipping problems, we encounter the same quirky market conditions, and we frequently eat and drink together. It's a privilege working alongside them. We thank them all.

The book production is another matter. There are two people above all who deserve our thanks—Detta Penna and Liam Regan. Detta gave freely of her design experience and instilled a sense of style and order to this book, while Liam gave freely of his printing and typography expertise. Thank-you Detta and Liam.

Russ and Shirley Searle

TABLE OF CONTENTS

INTRODUCTION   1

CHECKING THE COMPETITION
   Market research   9

BEST FOOT FORWARD
   Applying for a show   17

STRUT YOUR STUFF
   Show setup   23

SMOOTH TALKIN'
   Selling your work   45

GET YOUR BEAUTY SLEEP
   Personal attitude & health   61

THE GOLDEN RULE
   Craft show etiquette   65

COUNTING THE BEANS
   The financial aspect   71

APPENDICES
   A   *Sample business plan*   83
   B   *Costing and Profit sheets*   85
   C   *Display options*   87
   D   *Show Checklist*   89

The customer is our reason for being here.

INTRODUCTION

If you've picked up this booklet, it's likely you're a handcrafter who has had positive feedback from family and friends, such as "Wow! You could make a fortune selling these." But how do you turn a hobby into a business? Well, the best way is to enter small shows such as your local farmers' market, church or school bazaars, or flea markets, and then work up to larger shows based on your success. Along the way you're bound to have one or two shows which are less than gratifying, but don't think you've failed when this happens. You'll note that we said *when* it happens, not *if*. That's because even the most experienced crafters occasionally have a bad show. Sometimes it's due to lack of traffic, and sometimes it's due to your product not being suitable for a particular market. (For example, which would be a better place to sell garden ornaments—a rodeo or a home show?)

If you have a bad show, don't give up. Making and selling your own crafts is a rewarding endeavour—you make money, new friends, and gain the admiration of your friends and family. So it's worth it to persevere. If you have a good product at a good price, you *will* succeed.

Entering work in a show where crafts are sold, either retail or wholesale, can be a daunting experience for any crafter. There are a lot of questions which can go through one's mind. Is my work good enough? Will people just pass it by, or worse, laugh at my efforts? How much should I charge for it? Is the show juried, and if so, what criteria do the show's organizers use to compare my work with that of other entrants? How do I send in an application and samples of my work so I have a good chance of being accepted? How do I build a booth, or should I just use the tables provided? Do I have to sell to people, or will they just buy my work? What should I wear? What should I bring with me? Do I need a cash register? Do I need to charge tax? What are the various types of shows I can sell at, and which one is the best for me and my product?

These are just a few of the questions you may have when contemplating selling your work, yet it is very rewarding when these questions have been answered and you're enjoying a successful show. You get monetary rewards as well as pats on the back. Your friends and family are impressed with your skill and bravery in going out in public and showing your creations to the world, and your customers marvel at your skill as a craftsperson.

You also get to know many people in the crafts world and form lasting friendships with them. These are entrepreneurial individuals like you, many of whom have given up "working for the man" and work for themselves.
This book was written to assist crafters in selling their work at a show. Of course there are other ways to sell

your crafts other than at shows, but this book is not about internet selling, studio or home sales, or selling from a cart in a mall or on the street. There's nothing wrong with selling your crafts by any of these methods, but most successful crafters sell their wares at craft shows and markets so that's what we will focus on.

We'll show you how to avoid the most common pitfalls, and examine seven steps which will contribute to your early success. These are:

- Market research.
- Applying for a craft show.
- How to design and set up your booth.
- Selling your work.
- Personal attitude and health.
- Craft show etiquette.
- Bookkeeping and organization.

There are three types of shows where crafts may be sold: craft shows, trade shows, and wholesale trade shows.

Craft shows cater to individual customers who are looking for unique hand-crafted items. Some shows, especially the larger ones, are juried, whereas the smaller ones (eg. church bazaars) usually aren't. Craft and trade shows have different criteria for exhibiting. Trade (commercial) shows can be retail shows open to the public (eg. rodeos, women's shows, or home shows), or they can be wholesale shows open only to qualified buyers (eg. gift shows). Either type of trade show might have a handcraft section.

Craft shows, especially the smaller ones, tend to be more relaxed than trade shows. They can range in size from a local farmers' market, or church bazaar to a handcraft section at a festival. Larger shows, such as Christmas craft fairs, are frequently in major convention centres or arenas. Entry fees for craft shows can range from free to several thousand dollars, or you may pay a commission on your sales.

Your success at local, or smaller craft shows might lead you to consider exhibiting at retail or wholesale trade shows. Trade shows are always organized by professionals who expect the exhibitors to act in a professional manner. These shows are held in large arenas or conference centres and booth space can cost several hundred to several thousand dollars. Businesses that display at these shows can be importers, manufacturers, or crafters. Displays can be elaborate, professionally designed booths, or just a table and a chair, although the majority are well planned and appealing.

Wholesale trade shows are not open to the general public. Salespeople at wholesale shows are always well-groomed and ready to serve their customers with an order book close at hand, and smiles on their faces. Their job is to convince potential customers (store owners, service providers, and buyers for chain stores) that their product will sell and make money for them. Frequently these shows have a handcraft section, and booth space in this section is often less expensive than it would be if it were on the main floor. Handcraft sections, however, may see less traffic than the main sales floor because they're typically off to the side, out of the major traffic flow.

Some wholesale shows include a handcraft section because many of their customers are looking for a *local* product which is unique to their location (city, state, or province); one which doesn't look like it was turned out by a factory in another part of the world. In other words, they're looking for a product which will stand out from all the rest. This is an excellent opportunity for crafters.

No matter which path you take, **be patient with yourself.** It's doubtful that you'll achieve success overnight. Like any endeavour worth doing, creating a successful craft business takes time and effort, so if you don't achieve instant success, look around, take note of the successful crafters, and emulate their style.

Introduction

Don't give up. If you have a good product at a good price, you *will* succeed and find your niche if you follow the guidelines presented in this book.

Synopsis

- The seven steps to success are: market research, applying for a craft show, designing and setting up your booth, selling your work, personal attitude and health, craft show etiquette, and bookkeeping and organization.

- There are three types of shows where crafters might sell their work: craft shows, trade shows and wholesale trade shows.

- Be patient with yourself.

Know your customer's
buying motives.

CHECKING THE COMPETITION
Market research

I love her designs! They're so original.

Whatever product you're selling, you have competition. Even though your product is uniquely yours, you're competing for the same retail dollar as every other crafter. Jewellery, clothing, food, fine art, and pottery are the items most often seen for sale at craft shows, but just about anything you can think of is sold at these shows as well.

Go to as many shows as you can, and check out your competition. Look at their products, their displays, and their prices. Get a feel for what the customers are looking for. **Put your preconceptions aside.** Customers may be shopping for good design or elegance, or maybe they're just looking for something different. Note those crafters who present a professional image, and those who don't. Do their displays look well-stocked or empty? Whose booth is the busiest? Are they exhibiting a degree of expert knowledge? Are the crafters looking after their customers, even if their booth is full?

Take a notebook with you and look for answers to all of these questions. Then write down the information you need to make your booth stand out. Don't be surprised if an idea for a great booth design occurs to you while you're doing this.

Whatever you're selling, make it unique, something customers won't find anywhere else. It doesn't matter what you make, there is always a way to make it yours. If you doubt that, just look at the clothing for sale at any craft show; each designer has her own distinctive look. The same can be said for pottery or jewellery. It doesn't matter what you're making, put your creative hat on, and make it yours.

When you're observing people buying, try to *define your customer*. Is she the bargain hunter looking for a deal, or a person looking for elegance and sophistication at a reasonable price? Is it the career woman looking for glamour, the grandmother looking for a food item or a gift, or is it the young mother looking for children's clothing, toys, or presents? Whoever it is, try to determine who they're buying for, and unobtrusively watch to see where and why they buy. Realize too, that customers' reasons for buying vary from show to show, depending on the demographics of the attendees or the season of the year.

For example, many buyers at Christmas craft fairs are looking for Christmas presents, whereas at a craft fair in the spring or summer they're more likely to be looking for a wedding gift, graduation gift, Mother's Day gift, or something for themselves. If you're at a trade show, such as a home show or a rodeo, you should realize that many people who visit the handcraft section are just passing the time. *Generally speaking, people go to retail trade shows to look—they go to craft fairs to buy.*

Look at the pricing of competitive products, but realize that *too many crafters undervalue their work.* They either don't charge enough for their time, or fail to take into account all of their costs. We'll look at the issue of pricing in more detail in the financial aspect section.

When comparing prices for goods which are similar to yours, make sure you're looking at other handcrafted products, not commercially produced items. Commercially produced products rarely have the variety, quality of materials, or the workmanship that handcrafted items have—which is one of the main reasons why there is such a demand for handcrafts.

Think like a customer when you're looking at a booth. Customers want to feel they're buying something of value. So look, and listen to see whether or not the salesperson or crafter is giving prospective buyers as much information as they want about their product: what it does, how it's made, what it's made of, and if it fails, or if they just don't like it, can they send it back for a refund?

You might also want to test market your product. There are lots of small markets where you can set up a display to measure customer response. Try varying your price or display, and see what happens. Some people don't buy an item unless it's right in front of them, so if you have something you really want to sell, put it at the front of your table or booth. Chain stores do this all the time; magazines, gum, and candy are always near the check-out counter because they are impulse items. Note too that some people won't buy if something is priced too low. They think it must be a *cheap* product; therefore it can't have much value.

Choosing the right venue for your work requires some thought. As we mentioned before, some products sell better at one type of show than another. Our experience has been that a booth at a retail trade show (eg., an exhibition or women's show) typically costs twice as much per day as a comparably sized booth at a craft show, and generates about half the daily revenue. Remember, people go to trade shows to look—they go to craft shows to buy. However, retail trade shows might last as long as two weeks, whereas craft shows are generally one-to five-day events, so you might garner a higher income at a trade show, albeit at a higher cost. Keep this in mind when choosing a show. Find out how many exhibitors will be at each show. Ask the organizer to give you the previous year's attendance figures. If the show you're considering is part of a larger fair, ask about the traffic in the section you'll be in. *The more customers who walk by your booth, the more you'll sell.*

When deciding between two craft shows, or two trade shows, crunch the numbers. Consider the projected attendance, the number of exhibitors, and the costs of entering the show (booth fees, travel costs, staffing, etc.). Which one wins?

Market research is an obvious first step to selling any product, yet we're constantly amazed at the number of people who ignore this essential step to success. They do so at their peril.

After doing your research, *draft a preliminary business plan.* We know this might sound like a lot of work, and that it's intimidating to some people, but it really shouldn't be. A business plan can be a simple one-page document or a complicated presentation, but it should contain four things: the results of your research (which will indicate where your product fits into the craft market scene); how you're going to sell your craft; how much money you have and how much, if any, you need to borrow; and how much money you expect to make. Note: if you're going to draft a business plan for a bank or financial institution, you will need a more detailed presentation including a projected cash flow and profit-and-loss statements. Whether you need to borrow money or not, you should draft a plan for yourself. There are many examples of business plans on the internet, so find one that suits your needs, or talk to your accountant. A sample informal business plan is included in Appendix A.

If you're new to selling at craft shows, be prepared to change your plan. Reality has a way of intruding with unexpected costs when you're starting any business venture. However, once you have a few shows under your belt, your business plan should be firmed up. Then it's just a matter of following it.

Always keep your mind and eyes open and be ready to change your display, your booth, your product, or your business plan, because as someone once said, there's a better way to produce anything—except children.

> The satisfied customer is your best business strategy.

Synopsis

- Check out your competition.

- Put your preconceptions aside when looking to see what sells.

- Make your product uniquely yours.

- Define your customer.

- People go to craft shows to buy and trade shows to look.

- Don't under-value your work.

- Think like a customer.

- Test market your product.

- Choose the right venue.

- The more customers who walk by your booth, the more you'll sell.

- Draft a business plan, but be prepared to change it.

BEST FOOT FORWARD
Applying for a show

Why should I pay a photographer? I know how to use a camera.

Craft shows are more selective than trade shows about who they will accept as exhibitors. To get into a craft show, crafters typically have to go through the jurying process where the organizers pick and choose who they will allow to exhibit.

It might sound self-evident to say so, but *it is not acceptable at a craft show to re-sell something made by someone else.* At a trade or wholesale show, however, it's quite legitimate, as long as you're not in a handcrafts section and passing off a commercially made product as your own creation. Weeding out commercial products from handcrafted items is one of the reasons that many craft shows jury the work of prospective exhibitors.

Almost all craft fairs insist that *the person displaying the craft be the person who made it.* Friends, family, and even employees can assist, but the craftsperson must be at the booth, so plan on being available most of the day. By the way, if you are accepted for a craft show away from home and you need help, or if someone who was going to assist you falls ill suddenly, ask the organizers if they know of anyone who could step in. At the same time talk to the local youth employment agency or high school, or ask other exhibitors if they know of anyone who might help you. One of the best employees we ever had was a young woman (that's you, Jillian) referred to us by a youth employment agency in a small town.

If you're an artist, some craft shows allow you to sell reproductions of your work, and some don't. The same rule applies to photographers and musicians; some shows allow these artists to sell their work, and some don't. This is because CDs and prints (both art and photographic) may be considered as reproductions, not originals. Some shows allow exhibitors to use purchased patterns and kits; most don't.

The most important reason that organizers jury the work of prospective exhibitors is to ensure that the workmanship meets their standards, and that the items for sale are original, high quality, handcrafted items. They want their show to be an interesting place for their customers to go every year.

The jurying process also guarantees that there is a balance of products in the show, and limits the number of exhibitors in the most popular categories. Space at craft shows is limited, and the organizers want not only the most original and saleable work at their show, but also an appealing mix of products.

Be early when applying for a show, and submit your application well ahead of the deadline. Don't wait until the last minute; it shows a lack of organization. Make a note of when the application is due, and what is required. This may include a deposit and payment cheque, product photos, booth photos, and samples as well as the application forms. Do this for each show. Then make a master list, in order of date, of all of the shows you're planning to attend, and a list of outstanding items required for each show. This file is also a good place to remind yourself to make hotel and travel reservations, and to hire staff if you need assistance. Doing this will provide you with peace of mind as application deadlines approach.

If you're sending samples of your work, be sure to package them as attractively as possible. A sloppy packaging job makes a poor first impression on the show's convenors. If you are applying electronically, be sure you've met all of the requirements, and that any photos you attach are of a high quality and within the file size specified. If you're applying to a show you've been in before, send something new or something they haven't seen. *All show organizers want the most interesting exhibits they can find.* It's sometimes helpful to include pictures of yourself in action in your studio or workplace. It shows that you actually make the craft you're selling, and are not just buying it and reselling it as your own—something which, unfortunately, is more common than many people realize. Also, keep a file of any awards you've received for your work, or for your booth, as well as any articles which mention what you do, and include this information with your application.

Have someone review your application to look for obvious errors; after all, it's your first opportunity to put your best foot forward. If you are turned down, try not to take it personally; it happens to everyone at one time or another. Take a good look at your presentation and product line; revise and improve it, and try again next year. And the next year, and the next year, etc.

When you are accepted into a show away from home, and if you can't stay with family or friends, immediately make any travel arrangements you might require. You can frequently get better travel deals by booking early, and the hotels you want to stay at will probably have rooms available. In addition, many of the larger shows book blocks of rooms at several hotels for their exhibitors, but they fill up fast so don't delay in making reservations. If you will be using the services of a freight company to get your product to the show, be sure to get more than one quote. You should also ask the show organizers if they have made a deal with a preferred carrier who will give the exhibitors at their show a discounted rate.

Synopsis

- It's not acceptable to sell a commercial product or to re-sell something made by someone else, and pass it off as your own.

- The person displaying the craft should be the person who made it, although it is acceptable to have assistance both in the making and the selling.

- Some shows allow artists, musicians, and photographers to sell copies of their work; some don't.

- Jurying is done to weed out commercial products, maintain high standards, provide a good product mix for a show, limit numbers in popular categories and provide customers with fresh new products every year.

- When applying for a show, pay attention to deadlines and show requirements.

STRUT YOUR STUFF
Show setup

"Look at all the people in that booth. Let's see what's going on."

23

When planning for a craft show you need to decide whether you're going to design a booth or just use a table. Which is the best way to go? Well I'm biased because I don't like it when anything gets between me and my customers. *Tables can be a barrier*, and while there's a level of nervous comfort for novice sellers being behind a table, it's not usually a good place to connect with customers. It's not inviting, and it tends to enable potential customers to walk quickly past your location. However, sometimes it's necessary to have a table if, for example, you're selling products which need to be demonstrated, such as food or toys. In those situations you want people to sample or try your product, and a table makes sense. But consider your options before deciding on a table as the best choice.

On the other hand, most small shows are set up to be table shows, and it's the easiest way to get your feet wet. In small shows, where space is at a premium, it might even be the best way to go. Typically you will be provided with an eight-foot by thirty-inch table, but if you want more design flexibility, you may choose to bring your own. If you must use a table, it doesn't necessarily have to block access to your booth since it can be put in the back of your space. Nor does it have to be a large table—a small table might work just as well. That being said, a small booth without a table, and with your product displayed on grid wall, or shelves, can be built even in an eight-foot by five-foot space.

If you're going to use a table, *find some way to elevate your product* by using risers so the display is higher than the level of the table. Try not to make your customers bend over to see your display. Risers can also be used to give your display multiple levels. Go shopping for interesting shapes and structures—old tea crates, wicker baskets, wooden planks. Even cement blocks can be used to create an interesting display. Cover your risers with a cloth, and presto—instant table display. If you're fortunate enough to know someone with carpentry skills, you can have a display built for you, preferably one which is modular, easily dismantled, and easy to transport. Also, shops that sell plastic panels have pre-made acrylic boxes and if you need something non-standard, they can usually custom design just about any shape you want.

You're a creative person so *put your creativity to work* by designing something that will fit into your space. Could you use two small tables instead of one large one, or maybe you could turn your table at a right angle to the aisle? Sketch it out!

When a table is the only option, we frequently join two pieces of grid wall on the table in a V-shape, and then attach them to vertical six-foot pieces of grid wall at the ends. This arrangement provides us with plenty of display space for our jewellery, which is packaged on cards designed to fit into the spaces on the grids. Another effective way to display jewellery, or other small items, is to have a horizontal display, raised to counter level (we've even seen some displays that use customized table stilts). The pieces can be artfully arranged in a bed of pinto beans, coffee beans, or rice (which can be dyed any colour you want).

No matter what you choose as a display medium, as a rule of thumb, the darker and less cluttered the background the better. However, if you're selling something dark, such as black pottery, or black and white photographic prints, a lighter colour or natural wood might look good. If you're selling kids' clothing or games, bright colours might be the best choice.

Tailor your display to your product so that the product is the focal point of your booth. Place your table slightly back from the aisle so potential customers can see what you're offering without blocking the aisle. This means you should be standing beside or in front of the table, not behind it.

You can also use glass showcases which are available as freestanding towers, counter top displays, or full counters. These are often available to rent from the show decorators (these are the people who set up the show for the organizers). The problem with these is that they're usually expensive to either buy or rent, are cumbersome to move, and tend to dominate your booth, but they do give you a secure display space.

To add visual interest to your booth, *use the vertical space to hang banners or poster-sized photos.* You can also fill the spaces around your product with smaller photos, baskets of samples, or information sheets. Hanging poster-sized photos or banners up high also allows people to see your booth from afar, an important advertising consideration when the aisles are crowded.

If you have easy-to-assemble shelving, build your booth with it, and don't forget the background draping that many show organizers use to delineate one space from another. Many shows require that their background booth draping be completely or mostly covered. Think of your draping as a wall space for your message; you could have silk screened panels made which feature your product or name; attach them to the background draping supports with "S" hooks. There are endless possibilities for how you can use your "walls" to market your product.

No matter how you construct your booth, make sure it's not too austere, or it won't be as welcoming as you might like. Mirrors, a small pot of flowers, a dish of candies, lots of bright lighting, or pictures will all make a booth warmer and more inviting. Some other items we've seen used to good advantage include floor lamps, small tables with lamps, a Persian-style area rug, bamboo floor mats and bamboo curtains. Having said that, we've also seen the elegance of simplicity used to great advantage.

Professionally designed booths are also available. These set up quickly, and look slick. However, they also tend to look overly commercial, and both craft show organizers and the buying public expect your booth to be as "artsy" as you are. You don't want your booth to look like it was designed by the government to sell government programs.

If you do decide to have a booth professionally designed, look at the cost (they're quite expensive), and determine whether or not this type of booth is right for you. One of the biggest problems with these booths is that they usually have an unvarying footprint. In other words, you can't easily change their size or shape, and since booth footprints usually vary a bit from show to show, some flexibility will need to be built into whatever you order from the booth designers. For example, a 10 x 10 foot booth in one show could be either slightly larger or smaller at the next show, or you could be stuck in a corner of a hockey rink with a curved back to your booth.

It's usually easier, and better, to build your own booth. Common booth sizes are 10 feet by 10 or 15 feet, and may be on an aisle or a corner. Each type of placement requires a slightly different layout to accommodate traffic flow and your product. When you're planning your booth shape, think about your storage requirements too. One show might have a large storage area behind or beside your booth, and another might not have any storage at all. This could alter the shape of your display if you need to have a storage area in your booth. If you know you'll require extra storage space, make that request when you apply for the show. Organizers can sometimes accommodate this need, otherwise you'll have to look after it yourself.

As mentioned, steel grid wall is one modular solution to booth construction. Each panel is two feet wide, by four, six, or eight feet tall, and they're available in black, white, and chrome finishes. Stands are available (with or without casters) for the panels to sit on. They can be bought at any display fixtures outlet. They're sturdy and can be set up in any configuration you desire. We've found that cable ties (available in black or white), are the best way of joining the sections of grid wall together. They allow you to connect the grids at any angle you want, and cable ties don't cost very much. If you decide to use cable ties, take a pair of wire cutters with you so you can cut the ties at the end of the show.

A couple of tips when putting grid wall together: overlap, or offset, the edges when you're connecting them on an angle, such as a corner; it makes for a sturdier connection. Also, think about putting one at a 45° angle in the corner (remember to overlap), or use triangular corner shelves; this provides visual interest as well as making the structure stronger. Experiment with different shapes (curves, zigzags, etc.)—you can even build a three-or four-sided free standing kiosk out of steel grid wall. (See Appendix C for other display options.)

On the other hand, modular wooden shelving, available from various furniture manufacturers, might be the right solution for you. These systems have many options including clothing rods and slanted shelving, and can be painted any colour you wish. Or you might find that wire closet organizers are just what you need. No one solution works for everyone, so look around and see what's available.

Have a booth plan, but be flexible enough that you're able to adapt to the reality of the space you're assigned. Designing your booth before you get there (and that includes what you're going to display and how you're going to display it) will boost your confidence, and ensure that your setup flows smoothly. Some shows have height restrictions, especially for the first four feet back from the aisle; others have booths which are irregularly shaped. Get a pad of graph paper, and sketch your booth. Make cut-outs of the footprint of each component you'll be using in your booth, such as shelving or storage cabinets, and move them around until you're satisfied. Be sure to allow yourself space for handling cash and packaging your sales. You still might have to make minor changes when you get to the show, but this way you'll know exactly what to take along to construct your booth; just remember to take a little bit more than you think you'll need in case there's a surprise.

Take photos of your booth at every show you're in, then, when you do the same show again a year later (or do a similar one) you'll be able to see what you've done before. This can save you a lot of time. It will also give you an opportunity to critically examine and compare your displays.

Make a checklist of all the bits and pieces you may need including pens, scissors, stapler, business cards, product literature, etc., and put it in a "Show Box." That way, when you leave for a show, all you'll have to think about is your product and booth construction materials. (See Appendix D, for a sample checklist.)

Fabric draped on the back of an open-backed display covers anything unsightly which might be behind or beside it, and provides a backdrop for your product. No matter what you're selling, a fabric background will provide the colour you want to complement your wares. A word of warning though: the background shouldn't upstage your product. Refrain from using wild designs or colours for your draping, unless you're selling kids clothing or toys. You want people to look at your product, not your booth decoration. If you use fabric draping, the organizers of many shows insist it be fire retardant, and frequently require you to have a fire extinguisher at your booth as well.

If you're selling clothing, other than outerwear, build a small changing room or two, and have plenty of mirrors around your booth—you don't want two customers competing for the same mirror. Be sure to have fabric care and cleaning information on each piece you sell. If you're selling jewellery for pierced ears, supply alcohol wipes (available at any drugstore) so people can try them on without the fear of infection. If you sell food products, check with the local health inspector and the show organizers before you offer samples for tasting. What are the local requirements for labelling? Do you need to wear gloves or hair nets? Do you require refrigeration? What about paper cups, plastic spoons, and waste receptacles? You should have answers to all of these questions before you even apply for a show. Again, think like a customer. Mentally, walk through your booth with your critical eyes on.

We usually construct our booth in an inviting U-shape. This entices potential customers to enter our booth, just as we would invite a guest into our home—this is our space, but we're sharing it with others. *Another nice touch is booth flooring*; it can range from carpeting to foam tiles. We use interlocking two foot square foam tiles in a neutral colour, but they're also available in primary colours and in carpet form. This flooring can be purchased at most building supply stores. Many shows are in arenas or sports venues with concrete floors, and after standing up all day you'll bless yourself for buying the foam flooring. Customers like them too, as their feet also get a break from the concrete. We've even used them at outdoor shows on grass and tarmac. Foam tiles are lightweight, can be assembled to fit any size of booth, are more convenient than a roll of carpet, act as buffers when you transport your show, and are easily cleaned.

Speaking of cleaning, do it. Sweep your booth every day, or consider purchasing a small battery-powered broom vacuum cleaner. There's even a broom-style steam cleaner available for those stubborn areas, although a scrub brush and spray cleaner will usually eliminate any marks. A clean booth is much more inviting than a dirty one, and the floor is part of your booth. After all, you wouldn't want guests to come into your house if the floors were dirty. A less than clean booth can make any product look shabby. Or, as someone once remarked, if the carpet on an airplane is dirty, you wonder how well the airline services the engines.

You'll also need lighting, and the more the better. Halogen track lighting is readily available as are clip-on lights, both halogen and incandescent, but any lights are better than no lights at all. Just remember, that for any product where true colour is important (such as art work, jewellery, pottery, clothing, or just about anything, really); you need bright lights. Do everything you can to let your customers clearly and easily see your merchandise. You might need more than one track of lights, depending on the size of your booth. Also consider using the new daylight fluorescent bulbs that screw into standard clamp-on lamps; they might give your product just the right look.

Many shows dim the overhead lights, so take more lighting than you think you'll need; it's better to have too much lighting than too little. Lighting can set the tone or mood of your booth, so carefully consider the effect you're looking for, and be prepared to make adjustments as you do more shows. Calculate your total power requirements at the time you apply for the show. You can do this by adding up the wattage of your bulbs, as well as your cash register, and any other electrical items you'll be using. Many shows include power, but usually up to a maximum wattage; over the maximum you have to pay for excess power (if it's available at all). At one show, we were forced to purchase two dozen low wattage bulbs because we had inadvertently exceeded our power allotment. It's worth calculating this and ordering extra power if you need it when you apply for the show; it usually costs more if you are forced to purchase it on-site.

Have enough stock on hand to get you through the show; at many shows exhibitors are not invited back if they run out of stock before the show ends. There's an old adage in the grocery business, "Pile them high and watch them buy". If there are just a few tomatoes left in the box, nobody wants to buy them, but if those same tomatoes are put into a small container, preferably filled to overflowing, then they'll sell quickly. So if you find yourself running low on stock, have a plan ready to rearrange your wares to keep your display looking full at all times. As a general rule, *your display should look as full during the last hour of the last day of the show, as it did during the first hour of the first day.*

These are just guidelines, and I know there are booths that break all the rules and look great, but they're the exception. Remember that *your product is the first thing you want your customers to look at*, so whatever you do, make sure that it's the primary visual item in your booth. *Customers take only about three seconds to look at your booth*, less if your neighbour has done her homework and is enticing them to look at her booth—so make sure your booth clearly shows your product.

Large signage is also very important. Signs and pictures tell people who you are, where you're from and what you're selling. Some people are just curious while others see this information as a validation that you've made the products you're selling.

This observation brings me to photos, because many vendors supplement the visual appeal of their product by displaying large well-lit photographs of their product, or of themselves working in their studio. Everyone knows someone who takes good pictures, and it doesn't cost all that much to have them enlarged and mounted, so it shouldn't be a problem, right? Wrong. It will undoubtedly cost more to have a professional photographer do the job for you in his or her studio, but it will be *guaranteed to be right the first time.* The lighting will be right, and your product will look fabulous.

Look around a show to see which photos stand out. Phone a few ad agencies or print shops in your area; they'll know which photographers do good work. Get at least two recommendations before you approach a photographer. Visit their studio and see if you feel comfortable both with the person and with his or her work. Be sure to check the photographer's portfolio; a good landscape photographer might not be a good fashion photographer.

When you've decided on a photographer, plan how the photos will be displayed, and consider having your photographs and signs made all the same size and shape; it looks better when you display them. When you're having the photographs and signs mounted, have them varnished or laminated on both sides. This will allow you to keep your pictures clean, and to use them outdoors where it might be damp or dusty. Finally, consider having some or all of your photography done in black and white or sepia; done properly, it can be more dramatic than colour.

Whatever you're selling, it's worth your time to go into a store, or browse through the web sites or catalogues of businesses specializing in retail displays to see what they have to offer. This will help you to plan your booth design, and figure out how you're going to display your product, and mount your photos, and signs. Staff at these outlets can show you hardware which will allow you to attach pictures to grid wall or slat wall, or display clothing on a waterfall display. No matter how your booth is designed, you will need sign holders or clips to hold signs and shelf talkers. If you're using grid wall, one of the most useful clips we've found is called a clever clip. It's a plastic clip on a swivel with a split ring and it allows you to hang small signs or product practically anywhere. (See Appendix C.)

Go to as many shows, and as many types of shows, as you can. Take a notebook along with you and *go idea shopping*. Don't be afraid to ask the exhibitor where they bought that prop, or who did their photography—just make sure that you're not taking them away from a customer. Most exhibitors will be happy to help you.

Your work is unique, but has many display needs in common with other products, so look at every booth in the show, and decide which booths are best, and why. Is it the staff, is it the look, or is it a combination of the two? If it's the look, does it add to the product, and would it work with your product? Remember, *your booth should enhance your product*, not overshadow it. An elegant product needs an elegant setting, a funky product needs a funky booth—you don't want to send conflicting messages to your customers by having a booth display that is unsuitable for your product.

If you find you're booking yourself into more and more shows, and your hobby is becoming more of a business than a hobby, it's worthwhile having a logo designed. This can cost anywhere from a few hundred dollars to a few thousand, that's up to you, but you usually get what you pay for. As you did to find a photographer, ask around about commercial artists at print shops and ad agencies. A logo provides you with an identity that is uniquely yours, and this means potential customers take you more seriously. Make sure you get copies of it, in black and white and in colour, and have it put on a CD in a format you can use on the internet (JPEG or JPG, and PDF are the most common). This will allow you to do some of your own printing and to design ads, handbills or program inserts. You could also have your commercial artist or printer design a business card and price sign blanks. using your logo.

We've discovered that a home computer with a word processing program and a 4 by 6 inch photo printer is very useful for printing name tags, price signs, and shelf talkers that look professionally done because we can put our logo on them, or we can use our logo as a background watermark.

Shelf talkers are small signs that are placed in strategic positions around your booth. They are the "silent salesperson" that provides additional information for the customer: size, colour, material, ingredients, etc. They introduce your product to your customers when you are unable to do so. You don't want a customer leaving your booth out of frustration because you're serving someone else and can't provide them with information they want.

If you really want to annoy potential customers, don't put price tags on your product—it works every time. This is especially true at wholesale trade shows where buyers have a finite amount of time to see everything, a finite budget, and finite patience. The quicker they can see what you have to offer, the happier they are. Price signs should not be intrusive, but should be legible and brief. If you're at a wholesale show, be sure to indicate whether prices shown on your product are retail or wholesale, and indicate price breaks for quantities.

And speaking of product, *make sure you sell only the best of your work.* Selling your second best alongside your best lowers your overall image and makes you look like an amateur.

Don't forget to have a handout for people. At a craft show it could be a business card or even a brochure which lists some of your products. It may tell people what shows you'll be exhibiting in this year, or provide them with information about your product or web site. At a wholesale show it could be a price list or a list of show specials (note: show specials and markdowns are frowned upon or prohibited at most craft shows).

The last point we want to make about booth design is complacency. If you've been doing this for a long time, it's easy to convince yourself that your booth looks as good as ever, but *at every show you should take a critical look at your booth.* Step out into the aisle and see it from your customer's point of view and from different angles. Examine photos you've taken of your booth. Can people see at a glance what it is you're selling? Do your props need cleaning? Does anything need to be painted or replaced? Do you need a new backdrop? These are some of the questions every exhibitor should ask himself/herself because nothing retains its freshness forever, and a tired looking booth is not one people want to enter—no matter how good your product is. Your repeat customers admire what you do and always want to know what new creations you've come up with every year so *your booth should look as fresh as your new products.*

It takes a lot of energy and dedication to take your craft from great product to profitable business, but with commitment and hard work you can make it happen.

Synopsis

- Selling from a table can be a barrier to your customers. Booths are more inviting.

- Elevate your product.

- Be sure that your booth design suits your product, and never sell anything but your best work.

- Use your vertical space for posters or banners.

- Have a plan for your booth, but be flexible; each venue is different.

- Take pictures of your booth to remind yourself what you've done before.

- Make up a checklist for each show and a "show box" containing items you use at every show.

- Booth flooring is a good idea, for you and your customers.

- You can't have too much lighting.

- Make sure you have enough stock so you don't run out during the show.

- Customers take three seconds to look at your booth.

- Use professional photographers and commercial artists to give you and your products that professional polish.

- "Idea shop" at stores and craft shows.

- Make sure you have enough signage and that prices are visible.

- Always be looking to improve your booth.

You never get a second chance to make a good first impression.

SMOOTH TALKIN'
Selling your work

45

Selling is something I've been doing most of my adult life, and I've learned a few things about the art. That's right, *selling is an art,* but luckily for most of us, it's one *which can be quickly and easily learned.* There are three things every salesperson needs to know: good grooming, knowing how to listen, and product knowledge.

First of all, *see yourself as others see you.* This is called looking through the so-called third eye. Start by looking in a mirror. Are your clothes neat and tidy? Are your shoes clean? Is your hair neatly groomed? Are your fingernails clean? These might sound like simple details, but I'm constantly amazed at the number of people who don't concern themselves with their grooming. Don't forget, whenever you're selling at a show *you're on stage* so you want to look your best.

Next, try to *hear yourself as others hear you*; this is the second part of the third eye, or maybe I should say ear. If you feel uncomfortable talking to strangers, convince yourself that you're only "acting the part"— and eventually it will feel natural to you. Be welcoming and enthusiastic. Greet everyone who walks by your booth, and invite them in (eg. "How are you today?" "Have you seen my work before?"). You'll be amazed at the response you get.

Practise your *elevator spiel* in front of a mirror. What's an elevator spiel? It's a brief and snappy description of your product or service with emphasis on brevity—five to twenty seconds is usually as much time as you need. Tell your customer what is unique or special about your work. "Would you like a taste of our new mango chutney?" "All of my jewellery is made from argentium, which has more silver in it than sterling silver. The nice thing about it is that it's tarnish-resistant." "My fall and winter collection includes the popular new mid-length skirt. These are all my designs. Come in and have a look." Then give a very brief overview of what you're selling and where the different products are in your booth.

Are you sounding calm, or are the words tumbling out of your mouth like a runaway freight train. Are you speaking clearly and loudly enough? Do you look happy, or do you look like you'd rather be somewhere—anywhere—else? Don't worry if, at first, you're not able to be as clear and concise as you would like to be. Sometimes it takes a while to get the patter right; just persevere, practice, and it will come. This will be easier if you relax and enjoy yourself.

Let potential customers examine what you have to offer and then answer any questions they may have. Remember, potential customers are there to buy from you and want to see and hear what you have to offer so be clear in what you're saying, and look happy. *Most people would rather be around a happy, enthusiastic person* than a sad or angry one. If you're hiring someone to help you, make sure that they too are enthusiastic about your product. Enthusiasm is one of the traits which defines a good salesperson.

Never grumble about a show, or the hours, or anything to customers; they have their own problems and aren't really interested in yours. Customers in your booth want to be entertained, so take them away from their own mundane problems by letting your passion for your craft help them forget, if only for a little while, their own concerns. All crafters do what they do for a reason, and usually it's because they have a passion for their craft, and are proud of their creations, so let that enthusiasm come through. Customers respond well to passionate people.

The next selling tip is the most important one of all: *don't talk, listen.* The stereotype of a successful salesperson as being fast-talking and high-pressure is a false one. Successful salespeople briefly greet their potential customers, invite them into the booth, ask a question or two, maybe give them the elevator spiel, then they shut up and listen.

Pay attention to what the customer has to say, because that's the only way to find out what she's looking for. Ask her if she's seen your work before, or if she's heard about your work. *Then shut up and listen.* Being silent after you've asked a question is the most potent arrow in your sales quiver. People feel compelled to fill a silent void, and once you as a salesperson get over the initial panicky feeling that you have to say something to fill that void, you'll be amazed at what a customer will tell you. More importantly, you'll be able to tell right away whether or not she's casually interested or very interested in your product. Armed with this knowledge, you can then tailor your comments to fit her needs or desires. Maybe it's a grandmother looking for a gift for her granddaughter, or maybe she's looking for something elegant for herself. Either way, you'll know where to steer her in your booth and you'll have a better chance of making a sale if you've listened to her first.

Another way to look at this is that you're telling your customer about your product, while she's educating you about what she wants or needs. You need to listen attentively and respectfully (no matter how old or young she is) so you're able to find out what she wants. Maybe she's looking for particular dress, or accessories, or a spice, or a gift. Whatever it is the customer wants or needs, you won't know what it is until you first listen.

Try to ask a question that requires a positive response as opposed to a noncommittal one. For example, "Would you like to try that on?" is better than "May I help you?" "May I help you" is too open-ended and allows customers to quickly leave your booth

Be adaptable because your customers might ask questions about your product that you never realized were important (eg. "How do you clean sterling silver?" "Can this go in the dishwasher?" or "Is it machine washable?"). As a result, you have to be prepared to modify your introductory spiel to include what customers want to know.

Of course, you can't steer your customer to the right place in your booth if you don't know your product, but if you're reading this book you're probably a crafter who knows more about your product than anyone else, so you shouldn't have a problem. Just remember to make sure any staff, friends, or family assisting you also know your product. **Remember that many people admire your skill**, so don't be stingy with your comments about how you do things. Your explanation doesn't have to tell people where and how you buy your raw materials, or how you manufacture something; just give them a brief overview. Customers look at you with more respect if they know you make everything in your booth; so don't be afraid to tell them that.

One little trick you can use if your booth is full and someone new walks in, was taught to us by a friend who ran a restaurant. She said that when it was busy at lunch time, and she and the waitresses were rushing back and forth, she always made a point of greeting everyone who came in with a quick word and a smile. It could be as simple as "I'll be with you in a minute," or "Nice to see you today. Find a table and I'll be right with you." What this does is put the customer at ease knowing they've been recognized and appreciated, and there's a better chance they'll stay in your booth. If you don't at least make eye contact and smile or nod, they'll probably think you haven't seen them or that you're ignoring them, and walk away.

Unless you're engaged with a customer, greet everyone who walks by your booth. A smile and a "How are you today?" will invariably make people look at your booth. This might sound tiresome, but it really works because it makes them look at your booth. Of course, you can't do this if you're passively sitting in the back of your booth waiting for customers to walk in. You must be proactive.

Advertising is another important part of selling, but very few people actually do it. Some crafters think it's not effective and is too expensive, while others are intimidated by it. Well let us state right now that *advertising does pay off.* There's a lot of competition for the retail dollar, and anything you can do to put your name in front of the buying public will increase your sales.

The first thing to do is to figure out where you're going to be advertising and how. One of the simplest ways to advertise is to establish a mailing list of your existing customers, and send announcements of new products and show schedules to them. Repeat customers are very important in any industry. In the office supplies business, 80% of their revenue comes from existing customers, and while the percentage might not be the same for you and your craft, it's a good bet that many of your sales are repeat sales.

A lot of craft shows arrange advertising for themselves and their crafters with a local newspaper, radio station, or television channel. See if you can be a part of this. Another trend in advertising is to use the craft show's web site. Find out if the craft show you are entering will link crafters' web sites to their own, or, even better, if they have a separate section promoting their crafters.

Speaking of web sites, having a web site where customers can see your products and order from you has become increasingly important to the point that it's now a necessity. Not too long ago, personal computers were a rarity and the domain of young people. Now they're commonplace and most people use them to receive e-mail, pay their bills, and research what they're buying—and that includes what you're selling. Over the years our web site sales have gradually increased to the point where we can't imagine not having it. Hire a professional web site designer. Your son, daughter, niece, or nephew could probably set one up for you, but a professionally designed site will look much better and do a superior job.

If you're going to be advertising in a newspaper or magazine, it might be better, unless you've had experience doing this, to allow the trained staff at these publications to design your ad. Don't, however, give them loads of information to put into a business-card-sized ad. In every print ad, keep the message short and simple. We usually use a photo or two, our logo, booth number, and our web site address across the bottom. That's all that's necessary because all we want to do is to generate curiosity about our product and get the name of our business in front of people so they'll recognize it when they see the booth.

We're not trying to sell them anything with the ad; we just want them to look at our booth as they walk by. The booth and the product will appeal to them or it won't, but at least we made them look, and making people look at your booth is always the first challenge a crafter has to overcome when selling anything at a show.

It might sound ridiculous, but people can walk by your booth and not see it. Maybe they're talking to someone, or are distracted by the booth across the aisle from you, or maybe they're just making a beeline for a particular crafter and booth. It doesn't matter what the reasons are for some people not seeing your booth, you want to make sure that as many people as possible give your booth at least *the three-second booth look*. Advertising helps with this because it puts your name in front of customers. We know that advertising works. We can't count the number of times a customer has come to our booth and said "I came here today because I saw your ad."

Assemble a press kit: a collection of ads you've used in the past, any articles written about you and your product, a short biography, or a radio ad. It can be very useful when you want to advertise since you can usually adapt what you have on file to suit your current advertising need.

Radio ads should always be produced by the radio station unless you have a stock one in your press kit. It might cost you, but it's usually worth it. Just make sure that the radio station where you'll be advertising appeals to the demographic of your clients. Is it an oldies station, middle of the road, or a rock station? Which type of station do you think your customers will be listening to?

As for television ads, very few crafters have the funds to advertise on television—unless they can piggyback onto the craft show's ad. If you're able to do this, it's a marvellous opportunity to get your name in front of people. Some craft and trade shows are covered by the local media in an "about town" type of program. Ask the show organizers if this is going to happen, and if it is, can you be included in the coverage. Remember, if you don't ask, you don't get.

Consider using your packaging as part of your advertising. You could have bags printed with your logo, business name, product name, or web site address. All of this can be done relatively inexpensively, and it keeps your name in front of the buying public. Some artists and crafters even hand-decorate their bags.

If it's feasible, and if you have help, *consider working on your craft or product at the show.* Demonstrations of painting or making jewellery or candles are always popular because people love to see what you do and how you do it. It makes them stop and look at your booth. If someone was painting pottery or spinning wool, wouldn't you stop to look? If demonstrations aren't practical, consider hanging poster-sized photographs of yourself at work in your studio. Black and white or sepia photography can be very effective for this use; it hides clutter in the background of the picture and, because there are no clashing colours, it contrasts with the real world around you.

If your potential customer is shopping for a gift, let them know what your best sellers are. Grandmothers, for example, like to be told what teenagers are buying, and if it's a man buying for a woman, he's usually inclined to buy what you recommend. Whatever your product is, relate it to them; but you can only do this if you listen to them first. That's all your potential customers really want. Your listening to them will make them feel they're special.

Once the sale has been made, consider the notion that *no sale is ever final*. Tell your customer about your return policies. If it's a wholesale customer, can they exchange it for something else if it's not moving? Can your retail customer return or exchange it if it proves to be unsuitable?

Our rule of thumb is that anything that can wear out, such as clothing, has a limited guarantee against manufacturing defects, but all products should be guaranteed. Everything in our booth is "satisfaction guaranteed." If someone returns to our booth and tells us that a piece of jewellery just doesn't fit right or they don't feel good when they're wearing it, we cheerfully exchange the product, or return their money.

What this does is to generate good will, and in all the years we've been selling, that good will has created much more in the way of sales than it has cost us. Word gets around that we treat our customers well, and that keeps people coming back year after year. On the other hand, if a customer feels they've been treated unfairly, you can be sure they'll tell everyone they know.

There are always some customers who want a special deal. Do yourself a favour and don't do it. First of all, many craft shows don't allow you to put items "on sale," and secondly, once you start down that road it's very difficult to stop, and it can really eat into your profit margin. Whenever we're asked for a deal, our stock answer is that we give everyone our best price. We will, however, sell at wholesale to qualified buyers who place a minimum order, and when we sell to other crafters at our shows, as a courtesy we absorb the taxes (and yes, those sales *are* reported).

Having said that, you may choose to give quantity discounts such as "$20 each or two for $35" as part of your pricing structure. This can be a very effective incentive for volume sales. Just make sure that your profits aren't jeopardized by this. (For example, what would happen to your bottom line if everyone took advantage of your price breaks?)

Be sure that you *decide on your various policies* (guarantees, wholesale pricing, volume discounts, etc.) before you arrive at a show; don't make them up on the spur of the moment. It's too easy to make a mistake when making a quick decision. You also want to be consistent from one customer to the next and from show to show, because if you're not, your customers will find out, even if they live in a different province or city, and they won't be happy.

Regarding customer service, there are only two rules in business: rule number one, *the customer is always right*, and rule number two, *if the customer is wrong, re-read rule number one*. No one has ever won an argument with a customer.

Allow your passion for what you do to infuse your interactions with customers. People always respond well to enthusiasm. And never forget that *what you're really selling is romance*—whether it's tools or cars for men, or jewellery and clothing for women. Everyone wants to feel special, and what you sell to them will make them feel good.

> People love to buy,
> but hate to be sold.

Synopsis

- Selling is an art which can be easily learned.
- See and hear yourself as others do.
- Practice your elevator spiel.
- Always be enthusiastic and don't grumble in front of customers.
- SHUT UP AND LISTEN.
- Be adaptable; modify your spiel as needed.
- Greet everyone who walks by your booth.
- Advertising pays off with the three second booth look.
- Where possible, work on your craft at the show.
- Consider the notion that no sale is ever final.
- Decide on your policies before you enter a show.
- Rule no. 1. The customer is always right. Rule no. 2, if the customer is wrong, re-read rule no. 1.
- What you're really selling is romance.

To paraphrase Thomas Edison, *success is 1% inspiration and 99% perspiration.*

GET YOUR BEAUTY SLEEP
Personal attitude and health

Let's not disturb her. She looks exhausted.

For you to be at your best during a show, you need to be alert and ready to talk to people. This won't happen if you're not feeling well, so *make sure you get enough sleep*. Nothing drags a person down more than lack of sleep because your immune system girds itself for the next day when you rest at night. If you don't get enough rest you'll be prone to catching whatever bug happens to be floating around at the show, and getting sick can really put a damper on your success.

Consider getting a flu shot once a year, and be sure to wash your hands properly when you use public facilities. You might also want to keep a little bottle of waterless sanitizer in a discreet location in your booth. Bringing a second pair of shoes with you on show days is also a good idea—your feet will love you for it.

Drink plenty of water. Arenas and show buildings can be very dry places and your body needs water to be at its best. That's why schools now permit students to have water bottles on their desks during classes. Good hydration assists their concentration and learning, just as it helps you to do your job in a show building. Snack through the day, but be sure to have a good breakfast and a light dinner, especially when the show you're in ends past your usual dinnertime; a light dinner is more conducive to sleeping well than a heavy meal.

Show days can be as long as fourteen hours, so snack often, and whether you're eating a hot dog or trail mix, do it outside your booth. *Eating in your booth is bad form* and bad for sales; customers are reluctant to interrupt exhibitors while they're eating. Step outside the booth to a nearby rest area or quiet place. Some shows even have a lounge where exhibitors can go to relax. By going outside your booth to eat, you'll get some down-time to focus on your food, and your customers will only see you when you can give them your undivided attention. The exception to this rule is beverages. It's alright to have a cup of coffee or a water bottle in the booth as long as it's discreet and isn't in a place where you have to worry about spilling it. Just be sure you dispose of empty cups and bottles in a small garbage bag—keep your booth tidy.

If you're working your booth alone, consider finding someone who can help you when you need a break. Some shows assist exhibitors by having booth sitters available. It may be a free service or not. If you are unable to make such an arrangement, ask one of your neighbours if they will watch your booth for five minutes. Don't rely on them too much however, as they might be too busy to pay a lot of attention to your booth.

There are also professional booth sitters in many cities. These people attend craft shows for the purpose of providing booth relief. They usually schedule their time prior to a show, so ask your fellow exhibitors who they are and how you can get in touch with them; someone is bound to know of one or two.

Don't forget to balance your family life with your work. It's too easy to burn yourself out if you don't take time for yourself and your family. Make the time to enjoy yourself.

Your attitude toward customers should always be one of pleasantly rendering them assistance. If you're feeling alert, happy, and healthy, your attitude can't help but be a good one.

Synopsis

- Make sure you get enough sleep.
- Drink plenty of water.
- Don't eat in your booth.
- Find some way to get booth relief.

THE GOLDEN RULE
Craft show etiquette

"Can you spare a roll of quarters?"

Setting up and tearing down at a trade or craft show is something which can be a trial for anyone if they're not organized. There's frequently competition for dollies if you need to transport items through a building, or competition for space to bring your car in if you're able to drive up to your booth. Tempers can get frayed and it's tempting to push a little too hard. Don't do it. ***Be patient.*** You're going to have to live with your fellow exhibitors for the length of the show, so *give them the courtesy you would like to receive.* In other words, be calm.

Be organized when you pack and unpack your truck or car; this will be easier if you've made a preliminary sketch of your booth. Set up as quickly as possible, and you'll be seen as someone who gets things done with a minimum of fuss.

Check in with the organizers as soon as you arrive. Confirm move-in procedures and look at your assigned space before you unload. If something isn't right, it's almost always easier to fix it before you unload.

Whether you're thinking of coming back next year or not, it's a good idea to stay on the good side of the show's organizers. *Show organizers have one of the toughest jobs of all,* because they have to help find solutions to everyone's difficulties. For them there simply isn't any other choice but to deal with every problem, so don't be too hard on them if something isn't exactly as you expected it to be, or if something doesn't happen exactly when you think it should. They will address your problem because that's their job.

In all the years we've been selling at shows, whenever something hasn't been as contracted (eg., electricity not being available, or a booth next door that completely blocks ours) it's always been rectified. Be firm but polite—it works every time. And, *when a problem has been resolved, thank them.* Show organizers are like store managers who never hear anything except the problems or complaints; they appreciate a pat on the back now and then.

When you're building your booth, stay within your space allocation, and try not to block the aisles during set-up. If you do encroach on your neighbour's aisle space, ask them if it's alright, and offer to move your stuff if it isn't. Loud radios and strong fragrances also offend many people, so don't use either during set-up or during the show.

If you have a problem with perfumes, or an aversion to strong cooking smells, notify the organizers when you're accepted for a show. They'll do their best to ensure that your booth is not next to one that would make you feel uncomfortable.

Don't stand and talk to your fellow exhibitors when there's a customer in their booth, even if you're buying from them yourself. It could cause them to lose a sale. ***Do introduce yourself to your nearest booth mates.*** These people can be of assistance to you if you need a break to get a coffee, or just want someone to talk to. Take a positive interest in their booth and in what they're selling. Everyone has a story to tell, and people like to have someone listen to them (remember the sales rule about listening).

Don't go around scrounging for change from other exhibitors. They aren't your bankers, and, for that matter, try not to borrow anything at all. Emergencies do happen, but make an effort to be organized enough, and self-sufficient enough, so that you won't have to borrow.

Be sure to network with your fellow exhibitors. They will often share information about other shows, or tell you how to get things done in certain locations. Becoming part of the family of crafters can be one of the most rewarding aspects of your crafting career, and your fellow crafters and exhibitors will often become good friends.

Always open on time, and stay open until the advertised closing time. It enhances your professional image, and is respectful to other crafters near your booth as well as to the organizers. Sometimes staying open until nine or ten o'clock at night can seem like a waste of time, but whether you're right or wrong, that's what you contracted to do. Also, organizers take a dim view of crafters who don't follow their rules. More than once we've had the biggest sale of the day right at closing time, and that's because many customers like to see the whole show before they buy.

When it's time to tear down, be sure you know the procedure, and NEVER start to dismantle your booth before the show is officially closed. If it takes you two hours to get ready to move out, don't block the prime parking spot close to the back door during that time. By the time you're ready to move out, many crafters will be gone, and other parking spots will be available. Some shows have helpers to assist you with both move-in and move-out—use them; they know the proper procedures and are happy to help you.

Before you leave a show, seek out the organizers and thank them for the opportunity to exhibit. It's no different than thanking your hostess for dinner. If you have been given a form to critique the show, make sure you fill it out and give it back. Your feedback can help to make a show better. They won't know how you feel unless you tell them.

The golden rule is, *treat everyone as you would like to be treated yourself.*

Synopsis

- Be patient and give other exhibitors the courtesy you would like to receive.

- Don't harass show organizers.

- Don't talk to your fellow exhibitors when they have customers in their booth.

- Introduce yourself to your booth neighbours.

- Try not to scrounge from other exhibitors.

- Always open and close on time.

- Never dismantle your booth before the show is officially closed.

- Treat everyone as you would like to be treated.

COUNTING THE BEANS
The financial aspect

"If you're paying cash we'll just forget the tax."

Then there is the mundane, but hopefully rewarding, task of "counting the beans." You're operating a business, so *you need a firm grasp on the financial side of the business.* That's why you drafted a business plan when you started. Are you on target, or have you exceeded your plan? Or have expenses cropped up that you didn't anticipate? To know the answers to these and related questions you need to be organized and keep good records.

If you're not sure what records you should keep, hire an accountant to assist you in setting up procedures for you to follow. Then either hire a bookkeeper or do your books yourself. You might also want to consider taking an adult education bookkeeping course at your local college. Whichever path you choose, *your paperwork has to be organized.* Keeping an accurate record of sales, purchases, and expenses will make it much easier for you to assess the profitability of your business, and will enable you to meet your legal requirements such as filing tax reports.

As your accountant will tell you, you are legally required to keep a record of all of your sales. You may choose to use a cash register (new and used ones are readily available), or a cash drawer attached to a laptop, a sales book, or simply a sales journal (one line entry per sale). If you use a calculator, get one which can be easily programmed to add taxes. Be sure that all records are dated, and that any taxes collected are split out from the total sales amount. If you're living and working in Canada and you're a GST registrant, your GST number must appear on your sales receipts.

A cash register can be convenient as it provides automatic calculation of the sale, including taxes, and the amount of change owing, a secure place to keep your cash, and an easy method of keeping track of sales by product type. It also provides a "totals tape" at the end of the day to assist in balancing your cash.

Your copy of the receipts, whether you keep manual records or use a cash register, has the added benefit of letting you keep track of how many pieces you've sold of each item. This way you can tailor what you're making to what's selling. Maybe brown is in one year and out the next, or the latest taste sensation is mango, or dichroic beads are the jewellery hit of the season. If you keep sales records, do a regular inventory and keep records of what you've made, you'll know what's selling and what's not.

Don't forget that almost everyone these days uses debit and credit cards, so you should be prepared to accept both. If you don't, you'll likely lose sales; this is especially true of the larger shows, but we've made sales at our local farmers' market simply because we accept these cards. Yes, you'll pay a small percentage of the sale amount as a fee, but your increase in sales will more than make up for the commissions you pay. To put this into perspective, only 25% of our sales are cash; the rest are paid by either debit or credit card. If you use a terminal, an added benefit is that the transactions are instantly authorized and the funds are automatically transferred into your business account. Another benefit of accepting debit and credit cards is that you don't need to carry as much cash home after a show. This can be a comfort to you at 11 o'clock at night when you're walking to your car in a dark parking lot with the day's cash in your purse or pocket.

Craft associations and other groups frequently negotiate favourable debit/credit card rates for their members. These rates can really save you money. Keep in mind that credit card transactions require only a manual imprinter to process, but debit cards require a terminal for which you pay a monthly fee. A terminal also provides you with an accurate record of your daily charge/debit sales. This is a boon when you're tallying your sales at the end of the day or show. We use a small wireless unit that works just about anywhere (indoors or out), and which can be plugged in or operated on a rechargeable battery. Just make sure you get the latest equipment; the older models aren't as good as the new ones.

Many of the larger shows require exhibitors to show proof of liability insurance for a stipulated minimum amount; typically one or two million dollars. Even if it's not required, having liability insurance is a good idea for anyone who deals with the public, and an absolute must if you are selling food or personal care products. You should also consider insuring your stock against damage or loss, (at home, at a show, or in transit). Some insurance companies will allow you to add this to your homeowner's or renter's policy. There are also crafters' insurance packages available. Check with your crafts association, show organizers, or fellow vendors for information about who provides this service.

As long as you're running a business with a reasonable expectation of profit, *you can deduct all of your expenses related to producing and selling your product*; however, you can't run a business to create a loss in order to avoid paying taxes. Governments recognize that most businesses are not initially profitable, but there must be the expectation of profit.

Know the consumer tax laws in the province or state where you're selling. In jurisdictions where sales tax is charged, you are normally required to collect tax on all sales, (although some categories of goods may be exempt, eg. food or children's clothing), and to periodically remit what you collect. Even if you're only selling at a local farmers' market, you're probably required to collect and remit local taxes—don't assume otherwise, even if you're selling outside of your home province or state. Government auditors don't usually have a sense of humour about people neglecting to collect taxes when they're required to. Ask the local show organizers for information if you're unsure about what to do.

In Canada, small businesses with less than $30,000 in annual gross sales are not required to collect the Goods and Services Tax (GST). However, for those crafters who do collect the GST, they may claim the amount of the GST paid on purchases and expenses related to their business and deduct it from the GST they remit. This can be a sizeable amount, so it pays to keep accurate records. There is even a simplified method for calculating the GST for small businesses, so check with your accountant to find out which method is more advantageous for you.

There are many legal requirements you need to be aware of when you're running a business including:

- Business licences.
- Business name registrations.
- Federal, provincial, state, or local tax collection and remittances.

- Special permits, eg., food handling.
- Product labelling.

Review the need for each of these with your accountant or government office. If you're attending a show outside of the province or state where you live, the show organizers can also sometimes be helpful in letting you know which regulations apply.

Keep a separate bank account for your business. A business bank account may cost a little more, but it will help you to make a clear distinction between personal and business income and expenses. If you decide to use a debit/credit card terminal know that different banks may use different service providers, and you should choose the one with the most modern and trouble-free equipment.

Keep a close eye on expenses. If you're attending a show away from home, and aren't sure how profitable it will be, don't stay at a four-star hotel or go out for lavish dinners. It's tempting to treat yourself, but it can be very expensive. When you apply for a show, ask the organizers if they've booked a block of rooms at a local hotel for exhibitors (many of them do). This way you'll be able to get a room at a reasonable rate, and it's usually close to the show. As for eating, ask other exhibitors where they go. Some prefer to get hotel rooms with kitchens and do their own cooking, while others prefer to go out to local restaurants and usually know where the best food and deals are. We usually rent a room with a kitchen. This saves us a lot of money compared to eating at restaurants. The food is usually better and we get exactly what we want and the amount we like.

We briefly mentioned pricing earlier, but it's worth repeating here because proper record keeping will help you to determine whether or not you're making a profit.

If you paid yourself a minimum wage or hired someone to assist you at the same rate, would you be making money? You should be (although this might not happen right away), so include the cost of your time when you calculate the cost of producing your wares and remember—*you as the manager should be making a decent wage.*

Your retail selling price should, at a minimum, be double your cost of production. If you're going to be selling wholesale and retail, your retail price should be four times your cost. Wholesale customers usually pay half of the retail price (this is known as "keystone pricing"), so to make sure you still make a profit when selling wholesale, double your cost of production to get your wholesale price, and double your wholesale price to get your retail price. See Appendix B—"Costing Sheet."

The amount by which your selling price (either retail or wholesale) exceeds your cost of production is known as your gross margin and is the pot of money which pays for your business expenses. These expenses include those associated with each show such as booth and travel expenses, as well as expenses which pertain to your entire business such as bookkeeping, insurance, and office expenses. Your accountant will assist you in setting up the procedures so you know where to allocate costs and expenses. See Appendix B—"Profit Sheet."

If you do wholesale your products, but also retail them yourself, *never undercut your wholesale customers.* If you do, you will quickly gain a reputation as someone who cheats on their wholesale customers, and that's the kiss of death for wholesale sales.

Does the price of your product seem right? If your calculated retail price does not agree with the perceived value of the item, as determined by the marketplace and not necessarily by you, then you may need to make some changes. You may decide that you will only sell retail, or you may need to reduce your costs by improving your buying—which is something you should constantly be doing anyway. For example, are you buying your supplies wholesale or retail? You might also need to reduce your costs of operation, or, if none of these fixes work, maybe you should consider whether or not your venture is viable.

Good record keeping is important to the success of your business, so if you're just starting out, get advice from a professional accountant right at the beginning—it will save you money in the long run.

If you're organized you'll measure your success, if you're disorganized, you'll wonder why you failed.

Synopsis

- Organize your paperwork.

- Be prepared to accept credit cards, and preferably debit cards too.

- Don't forget all of your expenses related to producing your product are tax deductible, but there must be an expectation of profit.

- Be sure you know your legal obligations as a business owner.

- Keep a separate bank account for your business.

- Monitor your expenses closely, and always look for ways to reduce them.

- You, as the manager, should be making a decent wage.

- Your retail price should be a minimum of twice your cost of production and packaging. If you're selling wholesale, it should be four times your cost.

- Never undercut your wholesale customers.

Satisfied customers multiply and come back.

APPENDIX A
Sample business plan

Amy's Satchels—Business Plan

Premise:
Amy Smith designs and sews funky hand bags. Her product and business name is Amy's Satchels. She operates her business out of her home, and successfully sells her bags at a local farmers' market during the summer. Based on her success, she knows there's a market for her bags and feels she's ready to expand her business by entering craft shows. Her ultimate goal is to wholesale her products.

Products:
Amy started with a single product, her Big Bag, and has added six new designs. All of her designs have sold well.

Market analysis:
Amy plans to enter four local craft shows during the year. Based on what she's seen at craft shows, she has designed a modular display that works well at her local farmers' market, and which can be easily expanded for use at craft shows. Due to the unique design of her satchels, her market booth is always among the most popular, and she's confident this trend will translate to a booth in a larger craft show.

Funding:

Amy has been able to operate her business by using her own startup money, and more recently has been reinvesting her profits. To reduce her costs she wants to buy her fabrics and supplies at wholesale prices. She realizes that she may need additional funding to do this since wholesalers usually have minimum order quantities that are much larger than she has previously bought. In addition, she might need to borrow funds for craft show entry fees, additional lighting, and other supplies she'll need.

Summary:

This informal business plan is for Amy's personal use. If she was presenting a business plan to a bank, or any other lender, she would have to to include a detailed projection of sales and expenses, and would probably enlist the assistance of her accountant.

APPENDIX B
Costing & Profit sheets

Amy's Satchels
COSTING & PRICE SHEET
To make six satchels

Fabric	6m @ 12.00/m	72.00
Lining	6m @ 6.00/m	36.00
Thread	1.5 spools @ 2.79	4.20
Fasteners, zippers, buttons		8.70
My time	5 hours @15/hr	<u>75.00</u>
TOTAL COST		195.90

Cost per satchel (195.90/6) 32.65
MINIMUM RETAIL PRICE
    If not selling wholesale (2 x 32.65) 65.30 or 64.95
    If selling wholesale (4 x 32.65) 130.56 or 129.95

Amy's Satchels
PROFIT STATEMENT for GENERAL HOSPITAL BAZAAR
Nov. 5, 20XX

SALES
    Sold 15 satchels @ 64.95 974.25
    Cost @ 32.65 per satchel <u>498.75</u>
  GROSS PROFIT 475.50

EXPENSES
    Table fee 25.00
    Parking 10.00
    Lunch 7.50
    Wages for helper (8hrs @ 12/hr) <u>96.00</u>
  TOTAL EXPENSES 138.50
NET PROFIT 337.00

Don't give your customers what they expect—give them *more* than they expect. Bad news travels fast, but so does good news.

APPENDIX C
Display options

grid legs with levellers

clip strips

jewellery boxes

paper, plastic & fabric bags

racking systems

display cubes and towers

Photos courtesy Eddie's Hang-Up Display Ltd.
Toll Free (U.S. & Canada) 1-877-433-3437

Make Money at Craft Shows

grid wall

grid wall waterfalls

dressmaker forms

small easel

slatwall

clever clip

Photos courtesy Eddie's Hang-Up Display Ltd.
Toll Free (U.S. & Canada) 1-877-433-3437

APPENDIX D
Show Checklist

Your Office		Personal Items	
Alcohol wipes		Bottled water	
Brochures		Change of shoes	
Business Cards		Extra clothing layers	
Calculator		Gum or mints	
Cash Box		Hand sanitizer	
Cash register & tape		Hat	
Cello tape		Ice chest	
Clipboard		Lip balm	
Coin & bill float		Name tag	
Credit card imprinter		Snacks	
Credit card slips or tape		Sunglasses	
Credit card terminal		Tissue	
Note pad		Wet wipes	
Order Book			
Packaging tape			
Pens			
Scissors			
Show file			
Stapler & staples			

Your Booth		Set-Up Gear	
Anti fatigue mats		Asst'd hardware	
Bags		Asst'd tools	
Banners		Booth covers	
Booth draping		Bungee cords	
Cabinets		Cable ties	
Clamps & clips		Cleaners	
Display stands		Dolly or hand truck	
Flooring		Duct tape	
Gift wrap & boxes		Dusting cloths	
Hooks		Dustpan and broom	
Inventory		Extension cords	
Lights		Fan	
Mannequins		Garbage bags	
Market umbrella		Packaging tape	
Mirrors		Paper towels	
Posters & signs		Spare bulbs	
Racks & shelving		Step ladder	
Sampling equipment		Trays	
Shelf risers & supports		Vacuum cleaner	
Stool		Whisk broom	
Table & covers		Wire cutters	
Tarp			
Tent & pegs			

Notes

Notes

ISBN 1425177164